Carolyn Miller's
Sportacular Warmups
Book Three

Foreword

The purpose of this series is to increase the student's technical ability. Each book contains material designed to strengthen fingers, increase flexibility, and help the student master the many technical skills needed to perform. *Sportacular Warmups* combines sports and music. Students can relate the musical exercise to a similar activity in the five sport areas. At the end of each section there is a solo that is made up of exercises from that section. This is a wonderful review.

I hope your students will enjoy *Sportacular Warmups* and will become "Sportacular" pianists!

Carolyn Miller

Contents

I.
BASKETBALL

1. Lay Up

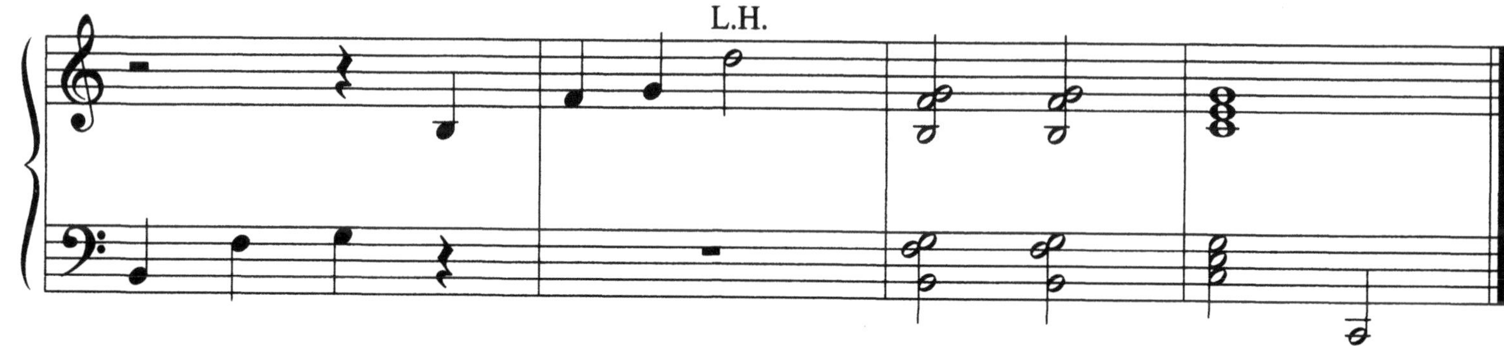

2. Over and Back
L.H.
L.H.
L.H.
L.H.
L.H.
3. Jump Shot

4. Over and Back Again

5. Traveling

Can you play measures 3, 4, 7, 8, 11, 12, 15, 16 legato?

6. Tip In
R.H.
Try different fingers for the grace note.
7. Three Pointer
5
1
1
3
1
3
5

8. Conference Finals

L.H.

L.H.

II. BASEBALL

1. Double

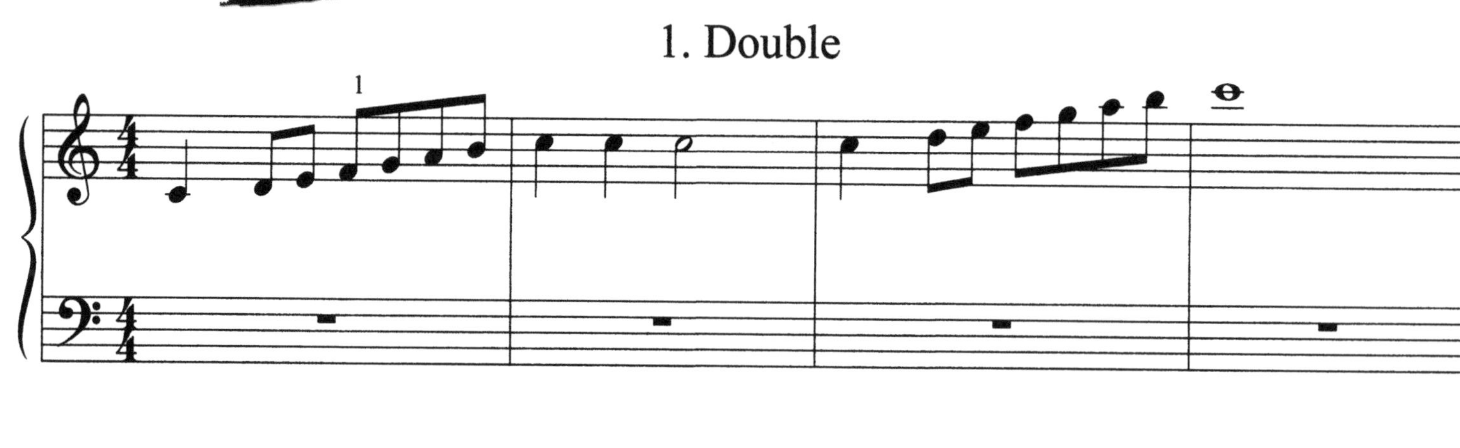

2. Home Run

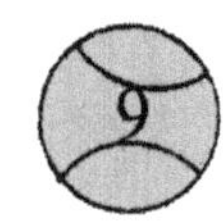

3. Scoreboard

4. Line Drive

5. Fast Ball

6. Knuckle Ball

Play with knuckles.

8va

7. Sinker
8. Curve

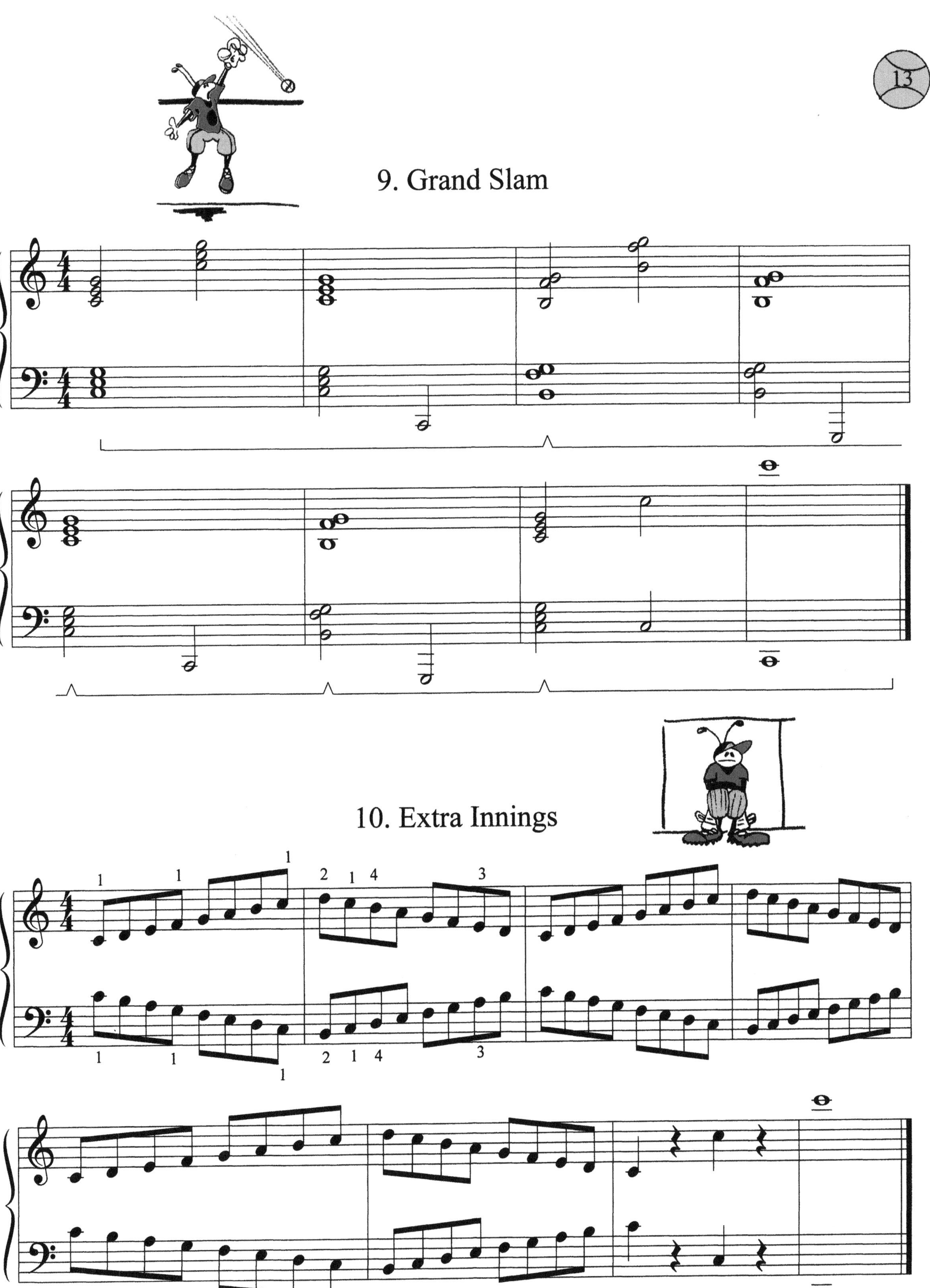
9. Grand Slam
10. Extra Innings
1
1
1
2 1 4
3
1
1
1
2 1 4
3

11. Playoffs

1
2
1
2 1 4
3
1
4
2
4
2
4
2
3
5
2
4
2
4
2
4
8va
3
3
3
3
L.H.
3
L.H.
L.H.
3

III.
TRACK AND FIELD

1. Warm-Ups

2. Twenty-Yard Dash

Which group can run faster, right hand fingers 123, 234, or 345?
Starting and octave lower, try left hand fingers 321, 432, 543.

3. Hurdles

4. More Hurdles
5. Starting Gun
Race #1
8va
Race #2
left hand only

Can you play the "Tug of War" so that the other side wins?

8. Marathon

9. Olympic Trials

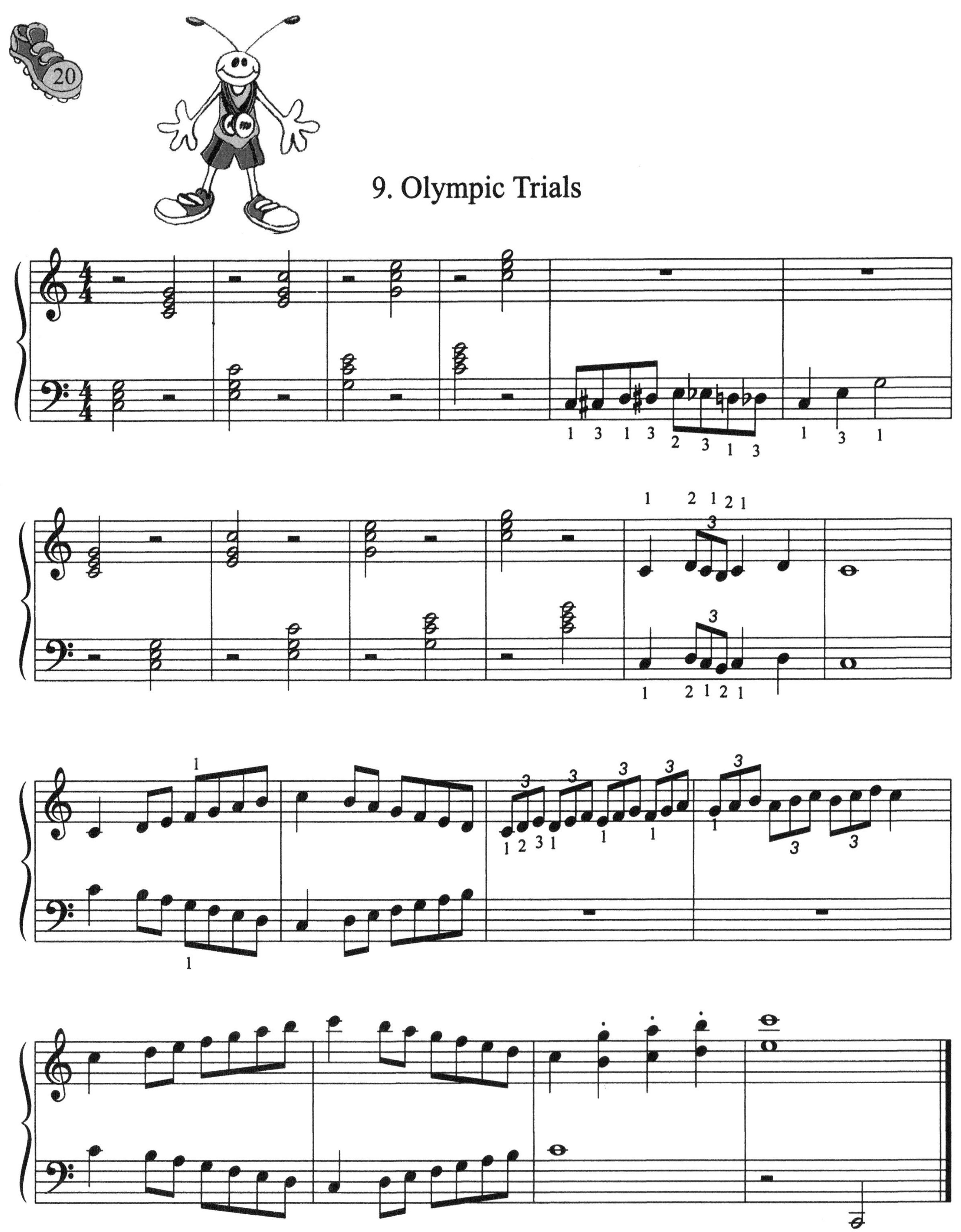

IV.
EXTREME ADVENTURE SPORTS

1. Getting Ready

1

5

2. Shooting the Rapids

1 2

5 4

L.H.

For more challenging rapids, change the E's in measures 9, 10 and 13 to E flats.

3. Hang Ten

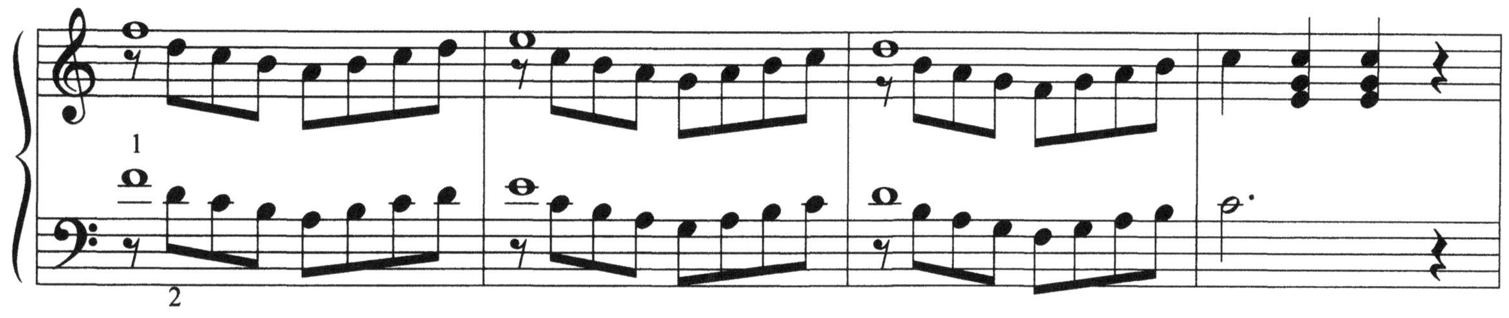

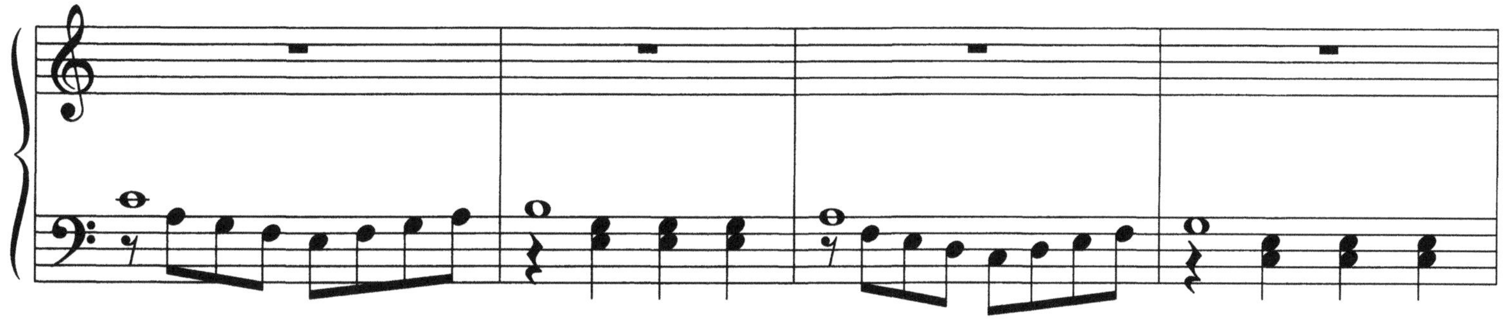

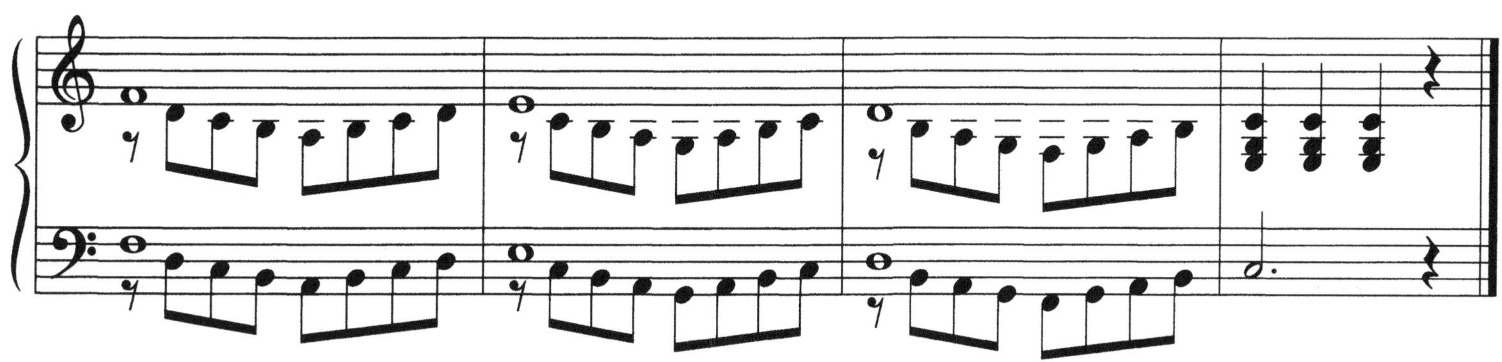

4. Wheelie

5. Double Wheelie

6. Free Fall

7. Take It Over the Edge

V.
SOCCER

1. Direct Kick

2. Corner Kick

3. Passing

4. Shoot Out

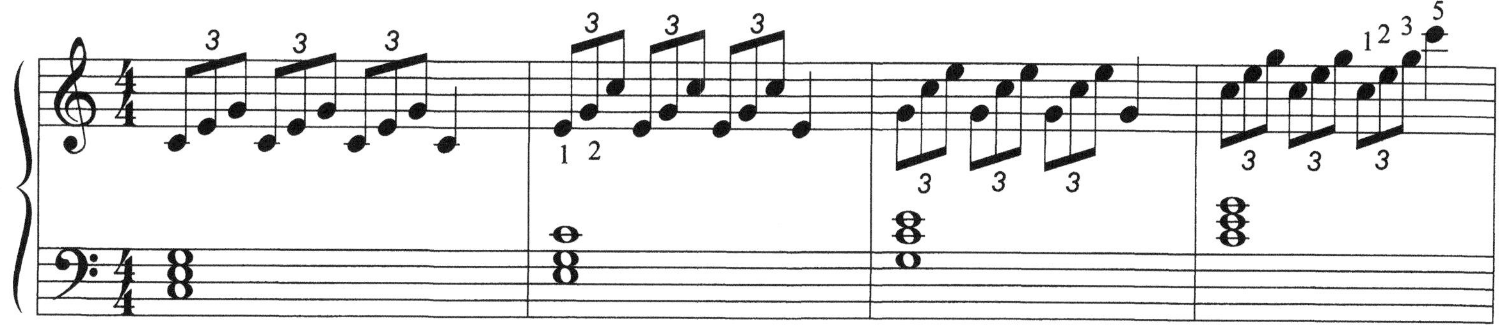

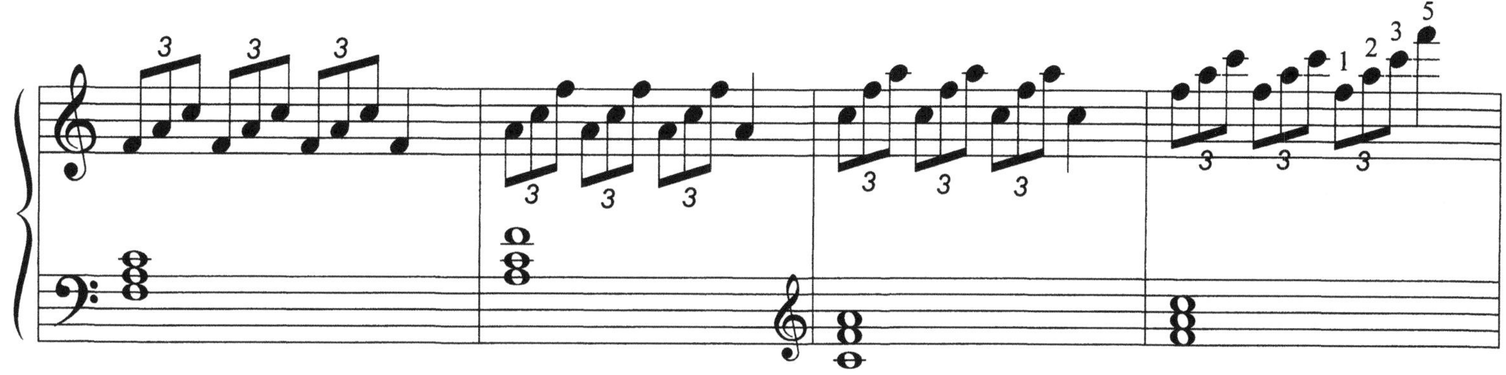

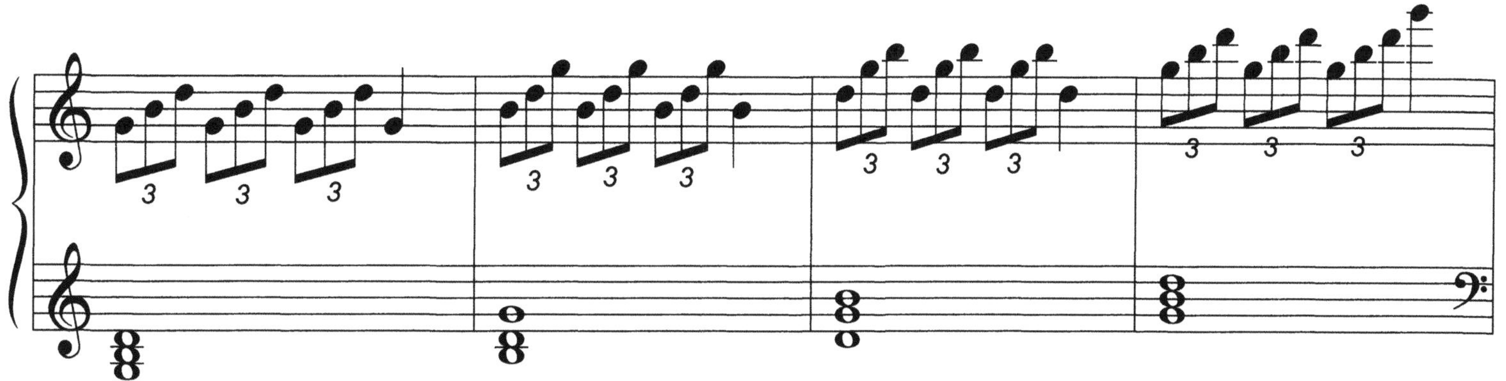

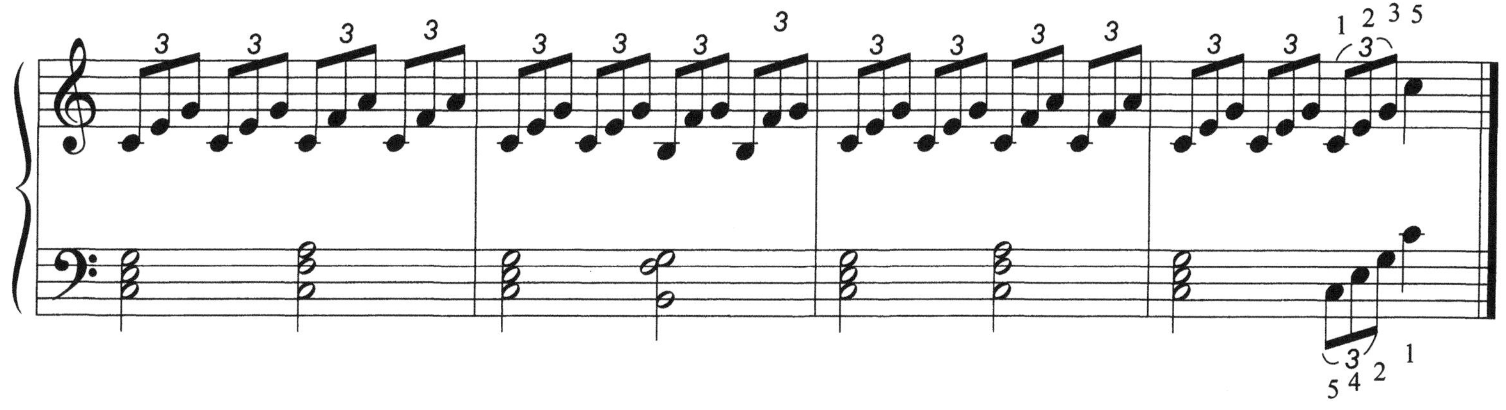

5. Time Out

12167

6. Goal Shot

1

R.H.

1 4

7. League Championship

1 2 3 5

R.H.